Building an RMF Environment

Jeffrey Lush –

First Printing: 2018

ISBN: 978-0-359-18595-5

Purchase printed book at: http://www.lulu.com Search for Jeffrey Lush

Contents

Introduction

With investments that approach the trillions, organizations continue to struggle with how to keep their environments secure. Many organizations are taking steps in the right direction, although frequently find the path of least resistance to be most attractive and acceptable. The path of least resistance or the "default approach" frequently involves establishing a secure perimeter, and monitoring for active threats through predictive analysis and vulnerability assessments, all of which are needed practices, and we are gaining some ground, although far from winning the war.

We've established "what right looks like" through the development of controls, policies, and regulations, although without accountability, provide little more than cursory comfort to stakeholders and little if any value to making environments more secure.

Cyber defense must be accountable and creative, as were the Continentals.

Unfortunately, throughout the globe cyber defense too frequently is reminiscent of the tactics deployed by the British during the Revolutionary War in the United States of America from 1775 to 1783. The British, one of, if not the most potent military of the time, created lines of soldiers in open spaces to wage war against the Continentals. The Continentals, hid behind trees and were very creative, eventually winning the Revolutionary War, a miracle measured by most. Cyber defense requires creativity and must be accountable, cybersecurity must be more like the Continentals and perhaps less like the 1775 British military.

Within the contents of this book, we will explore establishing a cyber strategy, morphing the cyber strategy into cyber accountability, and managing threat throughout the process. This book will focus on the US Department of Defense Risk Management Framework (RMF). Learning will be broken down into actionable comments with direct relationships to solve challenges to implementing a Risk Management Framework. We will walk through, step-by-step the crucial details and creativity required to win the cyber war as the Continentals did in 1783.

The strategies and discussion herein can be easily applied to any implementation of cyber defense, indeed not isolated to the US Department of Defense.

Chapter 1: Establish the foundation - Controls

It is impossible to declare success in the absence of defining what success is. Indeed, there is no lack of passion within cybersecurity professionals, which include professionals interested in cyber policies  and controls, or cyber professionals engaged in cyber operations. Each of these groups of professionals focuses on achieving cyber strength for their environment.

The challenge in the industry: Do our efforts result in a compliant data center and services? Are we making it more difficult for cybercriminals?

For some environments, a defined set of cyber controls and cyber policy can be a daunting task. There are thousands of controls, in fact within the US Department of Defense there are lingering controls from DoD 8500, agency-specific controls and policies, and other controls and policies all attempting to align with NIST 800-53 and other NIST standards.

CHALLENGE

How do we accurately categorize our specific needs and develop control language to satisfy our requirements (RMF Step 1-3)?

LEXICON

A *cyber control* is an objective and the implementation of the objective within the environment. A cyber control is very specific with the objectives, for example encryption, insider threat, and physical security. Cyber controls are often found within industry control bodies.

A *security framework* is a collection of cyber controls focused on control language that meets unique needs of a business vertical. Some examples include NIST for the US government, ISO for manufacturing, FDIC for banking, SANS for corporations and many others not listed.

A *cyber policy* is a foundational effort, the starting point for accountability within cyber operations. A cyber policy is the collection of cyber controls into an actionable state. Frequently throughout the US Government, a cyber policy is referred to as an Authority to Operate or ATO. Cyber policies are frequently confused for industry security frameworks of controls. For example, DFARS, a standard established for contractors serving the US Department of Defense, is a derivative of controls found within NIST. It is not uncommon to have multiple cyber policies specific to organizational outcomes. Within RMF, ATO's may be focused on human resources, the S3, and Units, Brigades, Battalions and Companies as a few examples.

A *crosswalk* is a mapping between multiple security frameworks. Many controls within security frameworks are very similar, the crosswalk enables organizations to see "like" controls.

Cyber control objective. The cyber control objective states the desired outcome related to the control.

Cyber control implementation. Using the cyber control objective as the guide, the control is "implemented" within the environment. Implementation requires technical expertise to fulfill the guidance provided within the implementation and control language.

INSIGHT

Use case example: 508 compliance and RMF

For DoD environments that have specific regulations that must be satisfied, for example, 508 compliance, an established set of standards are available. There are hundreds of applications that will review our websites, and analyze our files producing a visual representation of how well we comply with the defined policy.

If we are unable to make the rules and policy actionable, we can find ourselves spending more time than available to become compliant or accept the reality that compliance is out of our reach. In the world defined by compliance to policy, frequently initiated by organizations unfamiliar with information technology, becoming compliant now and in the future will become progressively more difficult.

Understanding the components associated with building a control, will allow organizations to optimize their control implementations, as well as other time and cost saving efforts. An environment can easily have hundreds of cyber controls, each very specific in their need and execution. The cyber control objective language should remain consistent as it supports multiple cyber policies within the environment. Remember, cyber controls are the primary ingredients of cyber policy, hence having a single control like AC-2 appear in multiple if not all the cyber policies for an organization, is not uncommon. Consistency within the control objective allows an organization to inherit controls between multiple policies.

The inheritance of controls provides multiple business and financial rewards. Inheriting controls allows for a control to be updated once and propagated to as many policies that have included the control. For an estimated 40 to 50% of all controls and policies, the ability to inherit allows the organization to establish multiple policies and save time and cost. As a control is updated, the update is applied once and because of the inherent nature of the control, is updated on all associated policies.

Rarely are two environments the same, the implementation of the control must remain fluid. To maintain consistency throughout the enterprise the control must stay firm and unmovable, whereas to meet the highly fluid configurations of a large enterprise, like the US Department of Defense, the implementation of the technologies needed to be compliant with a control, set of controls, baseline or ATO.

As you begin to develop controls for your policies look at the possibility of merging existing controls, perhaps some from other control frameworks, to create a new control to meet your specific needs. With thousands of controls available in the marketplace, rare is the time when you need to create a control from scratch. The ability to merge controls will save time, effort and money.

ACTION

What are some of the actions needed to meet the demands of the challenge: *How do we accurately categorize our specific needs and develop control language to satisfy our requirements (RMF Step 1-3)?*
1. Are you seeking regulatory cyber policy?

      a. Yes, the regulation will define a starting point for the controls needed.

      b. No, define a list of cyber objectives you would like in your environment. See the tasks section in this chapter for some ideas to get you started.

2. Now that the controls have been defined develop a crosswalk (see lexicon) to discover the shared strength of the desired controls found within multiple cyber frameworks (see lexicon).

3. Fine tune the cyber control objective (see lexicon) established and define the cyber control implementation (see lexicon) default language within your environment for all controls.

4. Create a control to policy mapping taking into consideration the need for unique controls, while others can be shared controls. Declare the policy and map the needed controls from your pool of controls.

5. Remember the controls will remain with a consistent cyber control objective language (especially the controls that are shared) and align the controls with the multiple cyber policies within your environment.

6. Review the cyber controls for each cyber policy and adjust the impact of the control as it relates to the cyber policy objective. As stated in the lexicon for the chapter, an organization will have multiple policies, and the implementation of the controls in support of the policy will be dictated by the impact of the policy within the organization.

ASSISTANCE

BAP and partners can assist in meeting your RMF and cyber objectives. The following "Cyber Steps" enable organizations to achieve Cyber Accountability. As an example, listed are the **BAP** and **RMF** Cyber Steps.

RMF Cyber Steps	Assistance available
Step 1: Categorize the needs to meet DoD cyber needs.	a. **bapEnterprise** (virtual appliance) and **bapCloud** (SaaS) provides a framework that will organize all your controls and policies. b. **bapOCS** (Objectives of Cyber Security) to discover the controls that are needed. c. **bapReader** enables organizations to look through existing policy and map to NIST 800-53 rev5 controls. d. **bapJumpStart** install over 4,000 controls in minutes to get you up and running quickly.
Step 2: Design and Implement Cyber Controls	a. **bapControl** allows for the development of controls in a Security Development Operations (Sec DevOps) environment. b. **bapStrategy** enables the development of the SSP, controls and non-technical controls to be validated for correct implementation language (see details in the next chapter of this book). c. **bapBaseline** enables control inheritance, sharing, cloning and merging for rapid ATO development. d. **BAP partners** aid with the development of the controls and implementation language, while taking advantage of BAP software for validation.
Step 3: Implement the cyber controls in the environment	a. **BAP Sharing** enables sharing of controls and policies throughout the enterprise. b. **BAP** extends deployment of RMF standards throughout the enterprise enabling a centralized development and replication to multiple sites

within the organization, while providing centralized deployment status reporting.

b. **BAP partners** aid with the development of the controls and implementation language, while taking advantage of BAP software for validation and preparation for RMF Step 6 – Continuous Monitoring.

GETTING START WITH CHAPTER 1 AND BAP

As organizations build their RMF infrastructure they can begin the process by inputting their controls and policies into BAP. BAP enables RMF control modifications, and the ability to inherit and organize controls into cyber policy. BAP software enables RMF policy cyber professionals to transition their efforts easily to cyber operational teams to provide visibility to the viability of the controls and policies created.

Discovery of Cyber Standards
Discovery of cyber objectives is a critical step to any cybersecurity strategy. With bapReader and bapOCS, organizations can quickly understand and build a list of controls and policies needed within their environment. bapReader can review existing policy documents and provide a mapping to NIST controls. bapOCS allows customers to select from cybersecurity objectives, leading the customer to develop a custom set of controls and policies.

Gain 50% more visibility out of the box
Following a successful discovery of cyber needs, BAP Jumpstart – RMF provides organizations with immediate visibility to approximately 50% of the cyber controls and policies implemented within RMF. Too often the hill to cyber accountability seems insurmountable, and we lose energy trying to complete all the controls and associated tasks for RMF, while the cyber threat continues to increase. With BAP Jumpstart – RMF we have preloaded controls, policies, and implementation language, providing immediate / out-of-the-box cyber accountability, accelerating RMF time to adoption. The use of BAP Jumpstart allows immediate results while providing the

work environment for staff to improve cyber controls over the course of time. Customers download the BAP Jumpstart RMF file and get right to work.

When pre-set controls are not enough
Sites can quickly create custom controls and policies from over 3,500 preloaded security controls, which includes all of the NIST 800-53 controls and enhancements or start from scratch to build their controls. It's as easy as BAP.

CHAPTER 1 SUMMARY

Start with a known and established collection of cybersecurity standards. The most significant collection of cyber controls is found within NIST, with the majority in Special Publication NIST 800-53. Regardless of your organization, the collection of standards within NIST is extensive and very impressive. Use the NIST control as a starting point for RMF and modify the controls to meet the requirements of your environment. Equally as important as building a collection of controls, is the management of the controls, the implementation language and the development of policy.

Save time and cost. When building your controls, use the correct tool.

Preinstalled cyber controls and policies within the application. The key to saving time and cost is to develop a set of controls that can be applied to multiple security policies, effortlessly, with a software application like BAP. The objective of the cybersecurity control is a known variable, whereas the implementation of the security control will be modified based on the security policy. Providing consistency within the controls, which for many environments will be hundreds of controls, is essential for all systems (a collection of cyber controls to meet a specific business objective: e-mail, database, files) you wish to secure within your environment. Encryption, for example, is important to multiple systems within your organization, hence the encryption standard will be a constant, whereas the implementation of encryption will vary dependent upon the policy that requires encryption: e-mail and web application.

The ability to share cyber controls and policies with others using the same application, enabling a centralized site to create collections of controls and policies for other sites within their organization. The ability to share controls and policies should be available for connected and disconnected environments and should always be free.

Maximizing time invested to develop the cyber security controls with the addition and correlation to the real-time threat to your environment. The ability to inherit a single cyber control to multiple cyber policies. Inheritance should allow for a cascade effect when changes occur to your controls in the future, saving you time and cost.

Chapter 2: Validation and System Authorization

Now that we have the controls developed with generic implementation language, we need to move the controls into the data center to enjoy the benefits of the policy efforts. The objective of creating controls and policies is to enhance the cybersecurity posture of the environments, hence moving through the process as quickly as possible is preferred.

Wedged within the creation of the controls (RMF Steps 1-3) we need to be prepared to "Assessment procedures for security controls" (RMF Step 4).

In many environments, an assessment is often a checkbox activity (see lexicon) that takes samplings, runs vulnerability scans, and performs a series of tests for control integrity. This level of testing is a significant first step although leveraging automation and artificial intelligence, assessment activities can be streamlined and validated against actual policy.

Validation of the implementation language related to the controls within the Cyber DevOps (see lexicon) activities will reduce time, effort and cost when implementing the controls in the production environment.

Many organizations are authoring the implementation language in documents or spreadsheets; a sunk cost. Augment the effort using the correct automation and dramatically reduce the time needed to complete Step 5 and Step 6 of the RMF process. The validation criteria can be authored by the cyber policy and cyber operational teams, producing a vetted system security plan (SSP)(see lexicon) and a clear path to continuous monitoring and RMF accountability.

Once the controls implementation, validation and policies are securely placed within an intelligent framework, validation, inheritance, sharing and continuous monitoring are natural evolutionary steps for the RMF environment.

In Chapter 2 we will discuss

- ✓ the effectiveness of validation techniques.
- ✓ review the authoring of validation key phrases (see lexicon).
- ✓ provide insight on building a firm foundation wherein cyber operations (see lexicon) and cyber policy team members collaborate to increase the cyber posture of the environment.
- ✓ introduce the impact of technical vs non-technical controls (see lexicon).
- ✓ the development of the system security plan (see lexicon) and required documentation for RMF Step 5- Authorizing Systems.
- ✓ and the automation and validation associated with data collection. Data collection is a key attribute for organizations struggling with overwhelming data management efforts.

The book will conclude with Chapter 3 that will review continuous monitoring and event management, RMF Step 6.

CHALLENGE

What is the assessment process for the controls implemented? (RMF Step 4)?

LEXICON

Checkbox Activity or Checkbox Compliance refers to compliance activities that are less than thorough. For many compliance activities due to the number of controls that must be validated, shortcuts are too frequently taken, the shortcuts are often called "system sampling".

System Sampling refers to a smaller representation of a "system that is being evaluated for compliance. Of course, sampling outside of this context has similar definitions.

Cyber Dev Ops or cyber development operations historically is the team that develops control language, control implementation language, and frequently completes and/or participates with the implementation of the control into the environment.

A *System* is the collection of hardware, software, process and people to provide a specific function or service to the organization. A system may also be referred to as a baseline or an ATO.

System security plan (SSP) is a collection of documentation that illustrates a system owner, the controls implemented and their relationship to enhancing the security of the system, multiple process-based documentation to include change management and configuration management. The system security plan also includes multiple levels of risk assessment and documentation. The SSP is the centralized collection point of all data artifacts associated with the system authorization and configuration from a cyber security perspective.

An *ATO or Authorization to Operate* is a formal declaration from the approving authority for the organization that the system meets security standards and is ready for production. The approving authority assumes the risk associated with the system. An ATO may also be referred by some as an Authority to Operate.

Cyber Operations are typically associated with the operations of cyber within a production environment. Cyber operations personnel may also participate with the implementation of controls. Cyber Dev Ops may be part of the cyber operations team in some organizations. Cyber operations may also include threat assessors, security operations Center staff (SOC) and others focused on operational tasks associated with cyber.

Cyber process and policy teams historically defined controls, build policies, and govern the validity of the cyber infrastructure within the organization.

Technical controls are frequently associated with components of the system (primarily hardware and software) that generate an event log.

Non-technical controls are typically focused on process-based information management like access control policy, change

Collection of data from internal and external sources

The collection and management of information both internally and externally is a difficult task, for most organizations there are 2 types of data collection:

- One time or re-occurring collection of information often referred to as "data calls"
- Regulatory collection required for compliance activities to include RMF, PII, PCI, NERC and many compliance activities that may be outside the scope of RMF

Efficiencies and cost savings are recognized as organizations leverage technology to assist with the process.

Common tasks for data collection

Multiple device collection.

When information is distributed does the recipient have to use specific software to respond? The cost should be calculated for the software required. Convenience is an indirect cost based on the value of the data as it impacts additional cost or revenue streams within the organization.

Distribute/Collect/Manage

Information in a highly secure and network isolated environment. What is the value of information within sensitive areas?

Immediate User Feedback

For the recipient of the interview to be more accurate in their response, inadvertently lowering cost, increasing the "usability" of the data received, and increasing collection times.

Enterprise visibility of the data collected.

The strength of the information collection is dependent on the ability to see all responses collected for a single site or for the enterprise. Data Collection technology should include:

- *Copy / Re-Use*
  Solutions must provide the ability to copy, edit, delete, clone and use parts of past data collections.

- *Locate files.*
  Ability to find data collections quickly in a structure environment.

- *Build custom data collections*
  Allows 100% flexibility as to the information collected.

- *Distribute data collections*
  Via social media, text message or email.

- *Validate and re-certify*
  The accuracy of the data collected – Validate. Provide feedback so that the recipient can improve their data input. Extend data collection leveraging technology to dramatically reduce cost and increase functionality within any environment, from business to the government.

Cost of data collection

To understand the cost of data collection and regulatory certification we need to assign time to each of the common tasks. Understanding this information allows us to get cost comparison to current labor intensive tasks within our organization. There is a real cost associated with data collection and automation can save cost while adding validation and accountability, without increasing your budget spend.

Cost per data collection task	Labor hours for data call	Automation used- Labor hours for data call
Correlate real-time events to collection	0	0

Copy / re-use data collected from the past	.5	.33
Locate files for the collection	.5	.08
Build custom data collections	4	.75
Validate collected information	10	.5
TOTAL LABOR HOURS	15	2.16
Based on a 72k annual employee salary performing the work, the cost for the data collection	$600	$86.67
BAP Cost savings per data call		$513.33

Cost of certification

Cost per certification	Labor hours for certification	Automation used - Labor hours for certification
Correlate real-time events to collection of certification information	80	.16
Copy / re-use data collected from the past certifications	1	.33
Locate files for the collection	.5	.08
Build custom data collections	8	.5

Validate collected information	125	8
TOTAL LABOR HOURS	214.5	9.08
Based on a 72k annual employee salary performing the work, the cost for the certification	$8,580	$363.33
BAP Cost Savings per certification		$8,216.67

Your numbers may differ from the chart above. Perhaps ask yourself, if I send out a data call to 10 people, how much time will the effort require? We are very conservative and estimate that you will spend at least 15 hours.

Imagine sending multiple data calls to support RMF, mix in a few certification and re-certification efforts, and you will soon discover the opportunities for the organization to increase the accuracy and effectiveness of your data collection and certification efforts.

GETTING STARTED WITH CHAPTER 2 AND BAP

With an increased number of certifications, to include RMF activities and data collection efforts, organizations struggle with effective management and accuracy of data collected. Work a little smarter without increasing the current budget. Some things to consider as requirements. The data collection environment should support:

1. **Multiple device collection.** When information is distributed does the recipient have to use specific software to respond? Convenience to answer your data collection will have a direct correlation with the success of your effort. Make is easier for the recipient and you will increase your data collection.

2. **Distribute/Collect/Manage** information should be consistent and intuitive. For annual certification imagine updating the information quickly over the course of the year. Do not spend time trying to remember where everything is located.

3. **Immediate User Feedback** enables the recipient of the interview to be more accurate in their response, inadvertently lowering cost and increasing collection times. Proving immediate feedback and suggested correction strengthens your data collection and compliance efforts, progressively getting better every year.

4. **Enterprise visibility** of the data collected. The strength of the information collection is dependent on the ability to see all responses for the enterprise. Enterprise management, distribution, comparisons, dashboards and reporting should be the default for any data collection effort, and with BAP it is a default feature.

CHAPTER 2 SUMMARY

In chapter 2 we discussed validation associated with the implementation of cyber controls, as well as validation related to data collection activities. We shared multiple examples and critical attributes of solutions that are required to perform validated implementation and data calls.

For many environments, the simple act of validation reduces the required time to complete the RMF process by an estimated 20%. The most significant impact is during the implementation of the controls as there are many dependencies and relationships to other controls that are implemented in the environment. A common oversight can create a ripple effect throughout the entire infrastructure. Validation of the implementation language before applying the technology to support the control, within a development environment, frequently time already budgeted that is optimized using automation. There are many benefits associated with validation, although the ability to do the job smarter, more consistently, and in a repeatable manner is difficult to monetize, and frequently will reduce time already allocated for tasks.

Providing immediate feedback as to the health of the control implemented can have a substantial impact on the viability of cyber architecture. Within the test and development environment, before production, reports as to the effectiveness of the controls implemented may prevent a cyber incident in production, a proactive approach to cyber architecture and implementation.

Chapter 3: Continuous Monitoring and Accountability

Continuous monitoring is often enabled through algorithms looking for known threat patterns, or the analysis of unexpected behavior within the environment. The understanding of threat to the environment is a step in the right direction, although the results must align with existing security standards to provide cyber accountability.

Cyber accountability is the ability to visualize the impact of the cyber threat to specific services or system (email, GOTs database, mission control) within the environment. Some of the attributes of cyber accountability include:

Automation and artificial intelligence to compare a standard to dynamic variables in an environment to ascertain the viability/health of the stated standard

Provide accountability, based on actual events, to the cyber health of an organization

Use of weights, priorities and key phrases to cumulatively ascertain risk level scores related to any standard and the impact on related standards to meet a common objective, cyber risk being a primary outcome focused on resolution for non-compliant and risk-oriented events

CHALLENGE

Now that the controls are implemented, how to we continually monitor the health of the implemented controls to maintain compliance and optimal cyber defense.

LEXICON

A component is often a piece of hardware or software within the environment. A component represents a small part of a more extensive system. A puzzle piece is a component of the puzzle. In cyber, to often we are focused too much on the component when the cumulated total risk related to the system reveals a complete view of the actual cyber threat in the environment.

When the *component is breached* indicates that the security of the component has been compromised, or in other words, an attack may be imminent.

INSIGHT

USE CASE- RMF: An agency defines and implements security controls using the RMF guidelines. The agency installs continuous monitoring solutions for the firewalls, networks, and servers. The viability or health of the firewalls, networks, servers is established through policies and in some cases automated remediation. Immediately following an attack, the Commander asks, "What is the impact to the systems that we currently have an ATO"? A common answer:

The xyz component was breached
A component breach (i.e. firewall, router, operating system, software) provides a good first step to remediation, although what is the impact to the ATO? The key to remember is that a "system or ATO" is a collection of components. There is a relationship between all the components in the system, hence if a component is breached there is more than likely a breach to another component or components in the environment

USE CASE- RMF: A DoD agency, AVSD (Autonomic Vehicle Safety for DoD-(not an actual Federal Agency)) has 300 different components within their environment (components are hardware or software like network firewalls, operating systems, applications, and databases). Using the RMF Framework, AVSD has implemented 500 individual cyber controls supporting 100 policies.

With 300 different components and 500 controls, what is the cyber risk or impact of an event to the health of the controls? The breached firewall has a direct negative cyber impact on three controls and over 40 other cyber controls ranging from access control to mobility to encryption (see Appendix A for details).

The AVSD agency has invested in a SIEM and Log aggregator, although struggles with the ability to prioritize and understand the impact to current operations, as defined by several ATOs' in the agency.

Log Aggregation and SIEM

The use of log aggregators and SIEM products have significantly enhanced our ability to find that "needle in the haystack", allowing us to create scripts and algorithms to discover the threat to our environment. Industry recognizes the value in these products, although the effort required, often exceeds that of the traditional IT administrator. The collection of events fails to correlate with the actual controls and ATOs' in the agency and provide a limited view of the actual threat as illustrated in the attached drawing on the next page.

The impact of the firewall breach is not as simple as an exposed port on the firewall; the breach also increases the risk level of other hardware and software within the secured system. Because of the breached firewall, the risk level of multiple components increases, elevating the risk to the components within the AVSD system:

- The router risk score increased from a 2 to a 7
- The network switch risk score increased from a 1 to a 4
- The LDAP server risk score increased from a 2 to a 5

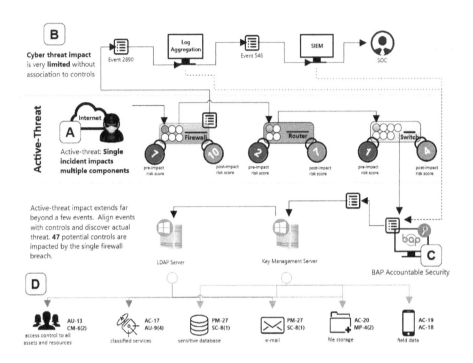

Continuous Monitoring

Continuous monitoring is the first step; which is frequently accompanied by the deployment of a SIEM Log Aggregation, and Cyber Operations teams, although to understand the actual threat to the agency, the agency must move beyond SIEM and Log Aggregation into Accountable Cyber.

The use of SIEM or log aggregators will reduce the number of events to be processed, although the mathematical algorithms needed to understand the risk level impact is very complicated, based on the staggering potential implications and varying levels of impact, controls, and policies. Build the RMF standards with Continuous monitoring as a top priority.

Agency Cyber Accountability is possible

Achieving cybersecurity strength is possible when organizations view the creation of cyber controls and policies as the absolute point of reference from which we measure cyber accountability. RMF provides autonomy at the local sites, although to gain strength must provide central management functionality. Agencies should have insight to the strength of all ATOs' deployed based on actual events in the environment.

Providing Accountability

Building an accountable cyber environment requires the correlation between active threat found in event logs to the controls and policies established within RMF. The hardware and software manufacturers define the events, NIST and the local command defines the cyber controls, both of which are known variables. As a result, the analytics engine can predict the health of the cyber implementation with greater accuracy versus looking for anomalies or other complex algorithms. As the event log produces a pre-defined and known error code, the event is aligned with defined security controls, providing true cyber accountability.

Event logs play an essential role to understand the active threat to the organization, to include sub-organizations. There are many ways to collect events from an environment.

GETTING STARTED WITH CHAPTER 3 AND BAP

BAP provides a unique value through the alignment of events to controls within the environment. The approach, called Accountable Security takes the SIEM and Log Aggregator to new level of efficiency and cyber defense.

Collecting events from the environment

Log Aggregators and SIEMs: BAP can collect data directly from hardware or as a consolidated log from a log aggregator and SIEMS. For large enterprise environments, a log aggregator is used to parse the tens of thousands of events into a more manageable event log before submitting to the bapFramework. BAP accepts logs from many different sources.

Push from hardware: a push of event logs is typically a server-side script or third-party product that runs locally on a hardware platform that collects current event logs and pushes them to a "target" directory, like BAP in a centralized location. Once the logs are in the BAP location, the BAP AI processes the logs.

Pull from hardware: a pull requires that a driver is installed upon the source server, and data is extracted from the source and replicates the data to a "target" directory, like BAP in a centralized location. Once the logs are in the BAP location, the BAP AI processes the logs.

BAP accepts data as a push target. BAP integrates with common replication software applications to move data into BAP for analysis. The BAP framework may also be installed in a "disconnected" environment allowing for patches, updates, and reports using removable media.

Manual feed of events for highly security

The manual update of event logs within BAP enables organizations to leverage BAP as an audit tool. Manual log updates are not a recommended configuration, as manual log updates do not provide continuous monitoring, although may be leveraged as an RMF inspection tool for commands and sub-commands and for highly secure and disconnected environments.

Cyber Health for multiple geo-dispersed locations

The phases of RMF are satisfied easily within the BAP framework. The objective is to establish a secure front-line and then to reinforce the front line over the course of time as situational awareness of the cyber threat increases. BAP is explicitly designed to produce immediate results while enabling the constant fine-tuning and improvement of the organization's cyber posture.

All BAP frameworks within the Brigade receives data from the Battalions for reporting, dashboards, and forensics. Fort Polk, Fort Sill, and Fort Hood all participate in a joint training exercise. The training exercise will include red team attacks on each of the Forts. Fort Gordon will monitor the health of the RMF infrastructure for all sites. The centralization of health status does not interfere with the autonomy required at each of the Forts. Data is encrypted and replicated to Fort Gordon enabling centralized analysis for the joint training exercise or specific health status of the participating forts.

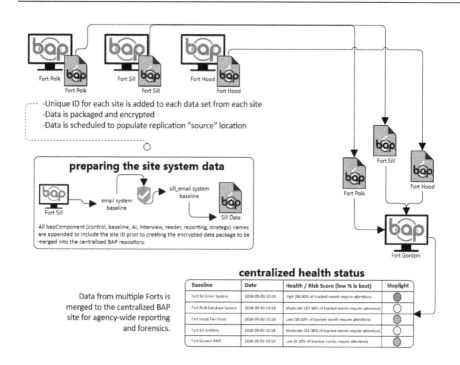

-Unique ID for each site is added to each data set from each site
-Data is packaged and encrypted
-Data is scheduled to populate replication "source" location

preparing the site system data

All bapComponent (control, baseline, AI, interview, reader, reporting, strategy) names are appended to include the site ID prior to creating the encrypted data package to be merged into the centralized BAP repository.

centralized health status

Data from multiple Forts is merged to the centralized BAP site for agency-wide reporting and forensics.

Baseline	Date	Health / Risk Score (low % is best)	Stoplight
Fort Sill Email System	2018-05-03 10:18	High (98.90% of tracked events require attention)	
Fort Polk Database System	2018-05-03 10:18	Moderate (57.10% of tracked events require attention)	
Fort Hood File Share	2018-05-03 10:18	Low (18.00% of tracked events require attention)	
Fort Sill Artillery	2018-05-03 10:18	Moderate (51.30% of tracked events require attention)	
Fort Gordon RMF	2018-05-03 10:18	Low (9.10% of tracked events require attention)	

As agencies identify and develop plans to address gaps in cyber analytic capabilities and risk management efforts, bapValidate, bapRemediate, and bapAudit can help. To address gaps organizations must first define a baseline that accurately captures their cyber objectives, for example, RMF. Then, using the BAP artificial intelligence and analytics, BAP draws a contrast between the actual state and the desired state.

Remediation and POA&M

Prioritization of cyber health is dependent upon our ability to focus on systematic risks that begins with the discovery of events as they impact defined controls and policies. Events discovered within the environment can be quickly prioritized using bapRemediate. bapRemediate provides a POA&M format as well.

Addressing the most significant risk first and focusing on the highest impact systems, assets and capabilities is a practical approach to cyber remediation. Remediation of risk is dependent upon understanding the direct and indirect impact of the cyber compromise. Once established, remediation efforts must be presented, organized and managed through the application of milestones, budgetary restrictions, third-party dependencies, assignment of resources and suspense dates. bapRemediate allows organizations to align actual threat to their environment against established cyber controls and policies, funneling remediation requirements for immediate action.

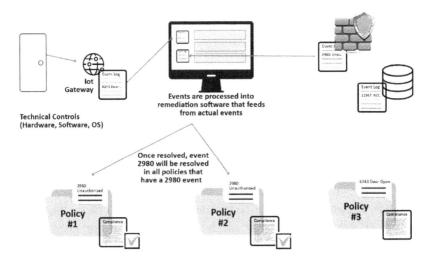

Integration of remediation functions, within a control framework, enables organizations to identify and remediate risk quickly. As events are resolved, the event should be fixed for all associated remediation efforts. For example, event 2980 is resolved and updated for Policy #1 and Policy #2.

Chapter 4: Calculate cost for cyber environments

The following pages breakdown potential costs associated with maintaining a cyber environment, although individual situations will differ considerably, the following should provide direction and guidance on understanding your cyber cost. The analysis compares cyber software costs that include hardware, software, the configuration of controls and their implementation, management of a security operations center, and remediation preparation for events that have occurred.

For cost comparisons related to cost, we will use BAP software as an example. BAP provides levels of automation that have a direct impact on driving down cost related to building and managing a cyberinfrastructure. Some cost savings are more specific to making a cyber structure, although even these environments have maintenance costs that will recognize cost savings through cyber automation.

Summary of cyber cost impact and savings

Included below are for summary statements representing the cost models defined on the following pages. Your results will differ, as there are too many variables to take into consideration when building cost models.

CYBER INVESTMENTS: Starting with the core infrastructure, How can you reduce server hardware, operating system, and storage costs, while providing automation to establish security controls and policies, coupled with maintenance accountability accelerating time to remediation.

SOC ANALYSTS: Security operation centers are staffed to address real-time threat. Within an environment that operates 24 hours a day, seven days a week and 365 days a year, explore how your organization can visualize the alignment of the threat to specific security controls, making it easier to remediate and prioritize threat, reducing the number of required analysts.

MANAGING THREAT: The average cost for processing events that occur daily within the environment involves investigation and remediation management. Cost includes investigation time to narrow down the point of impact and the tracking and management of remediation. As an example, if seven events occurred within the environment in a 24-hour period, and it takes 90 minutes to investigate (total FTE time), and 30 minutes to document and prepare for remediation activities, what is the cost to the organization? There is an easier way.

NON-COMPLIANCE FINANCIAL IMPACT: Noncompliance with cyber regulations will continue to have a negative revenue impact for organizations that do not enhance their cyber health and compliance. As an example, if your annual revenue is $1 million with 30% of your business from the EU and 10% of your business from the US Department of Defense, and you are found to be noncompliant, the first-year revenue impact could result in losses of 52% or $515,000. Year two is a little better with the loss of approximately $400,000. Although DoD agencies do not have direct fines per se, the impact for non-compliance can be severe.

Do existing Cyber Tools support my Controls? Can I make my existing cyber tools meet fluid cyber threat and requirements?

It seems like just yesterday that adding cyber protection to an information technology environment was an afterthought, an extra cost. Move the clock forward a few decades, and cyber security should be the first thought when designing or managing an information technology environment. Many of our environments leverage cyber technologies and strategies that are decades old. How do I know if my existing cyber tools? We continue to evaluate risk based on components found within the environment (i.e., firewalls LDAP servers, etc.). Perhaps we do not realize that cyber risk presents itself as a threat against the "collection of all components" within our environments, or what is referred to as a "system."

Do my cyber tools support my Cyber Strategy?

All cyber tools should support your cyber standards, policies, and strategy. If the cyber tool does not enable your cyber standards, a closer evaluation is in order. If you're looking to make a positive impact on your budget, evaluating the cyber tools against your cyber standards is a productive use of time and resources.

Can I see how secure I am, right now?

Information technology software is infamous for providing beautiful dashboards and reports of what the future holds for an organization. Although, like many software applications, organizations find the hill of education and integration too steep, and often settle for less than 15% of the software's designed functionality. For many cybersecurity software applications, like log aggregators or SIEM products, there is no doubt that the applications are rich in functionality and value. Is the value helping an organization genuinely understand their cyber health? Many organizations find the steep hills of education and integration for cyber continuous monitoring too steep.

The implementation and management of many cybersecurity software applications are demanding and expensive. Implementation times can vary from months to years, too often producing cryptic results that fail to align real-time threat with the cyber standards implemented within the environment.

Cyber cost is more than a single component

Evaluating the cyber health of an environment based on the independent evaluation of components (i.e., firewall, server, network) within the environment is a common practice for many organizations. This form of evaluation has merit, although in today's fluid and volatile cyber environment, as of 2018, component-based cyber health is just scratching the surface.

Cybersecurity threat must be assessed based on system risk, not component-based risk. Like the adverse impact of not carrying a spare when you get a flat. It is not just the tire that is impacted, the entire functionality of vehicle (or the system) that is at risk/non-functional until the component (the tire) is fixed.

Understanding the cyber threat or health of a specific component within the system is a good first step. Unfortunately, each component does not act independently in support of the business objective, or system. Contrary, all the components have a direct and indirect impact on the cyber threat or health of the business objective. This approach to cybersecurity is often referred to as component-based cyber security.

Component-based cybersecurity is a lot like evaluating the safety of your vehicle based upon the functionality of your spare tire. The spare tire is minimal, if any risk to the operation of the vehicle, although when combined with multiple events, can present a substantial risk to your health. It's late one evening during a snow storm:

- You do not have a spare tire
- Your cell phone has run out of power
- You realize you have no way of finding the necessary tools to escape the bitter cold; you are in trouble.
-

Cybersecurity efforts for our information technology environments are like the functionality of our spare tire. Component-based cybersecurity would have only revealed the absence of a spare tire, which would have been given a low to insignificant risk level. As the traveler, the inability to arrive at our destination may result in frostbite, hyperthermia or death; and the lack of a spare tire as part of the vehicle "system" now presents a considerable risk. Cybersecurity efforts must be calculated based upon system risk and not a component-based risk.

Establish system-based risk with alignment to defined cyber standards for an accurate perspective of your cyber health

With component risk levels established, when combined as system risk levels, if the risk is not aligned to security standards and policies designed to protect business outcomes, organizations will struggle to understand how secure they are.

Understanding cyber cost is dependent upon existing cyber tool cost, fluid cyber threat, visualization requirements, and component-based methodology for cybersecurity; all of which have direct and indirect costs. Following are a few ideas to get a better understanding of your cyber cost.

Infrastructure Cost

Implementing tools in a legacy environment. The figures below reflect a new installation of a specific or set of cyber tools. Adjust the cost of the line items to ascertain your actual cost. Calculating cost based on existing hardware and software is a difficult task as there are many variables to consider. When is the next refresh for the hardware and software? Are cyber tools sharing hardware and software resources or are do the cyber tools require isolated hardware and software? What type of operating system is needed? Do you have to upgrade from a "standard server" to an "enterprise server"? and the list goes on.

The following information is designed to spark your personal creativity in understanding your cost.

Existing / Shared Infrastructure – Sunk Cost?

The cyber tools in your environment are part of a shared or existing infrastructure. For these environments, it can be challenging to define hardware cost. Estimate the total value of the hardware resource and take a percentage of the price to support the cyber tool(s). Bringing you closer to a cost model.

Maintenance and Life Cycle Depreciation.

We can never underestimate the cost of maintenance for hardware that typically has the consumer pay for the software every four years. Although the hardware cost for today may be a sunk cost, the time will come that the value of the hardware will play a role in the cost of the cyber environment.

Consistency and Repeatability

Every environment will be different. Please use the information provided in the tables, insert your current information and define cost that makes sense for your environment. Consistency and repeatability will drive down immediate cost and provide the foundation to drive down cost for many years to follow.

Hardware to support existing cyber tools	Current	BAP	Savings with BAP
Cost for the server/desktop that is hosting the cyber tool	$18,000	$2,500	$15,500
The number of servers needed to support the cyber tools	3	1	
Cost of other servers (i.e. virtualization, database, key management) that are required to support the cyber tools	$20,000	$0.00	$20,000
Cost of hardware and storage to support the cyber tools	$12,000	$0.00	$12,000
Sub-total hardware cost	$86,000	$2,500	$83,500
Annual maintenance and support cost (based on 15% annual)	$12,900	$0	$12,900
Total cost	$98,900	$2,500	

One-time savings with BAP – Capital Expense	$83,500
3-year operating expense savings with BAP	$38,700
Total budget savings with BAP	$122,200

Software Enterprise License Agreements

Software licensing in larger environments may be part of an enterprise agreement. Hence the cost may be pushed to another group within the organization. The cost of the software should be considered when evaluating the total cost of a cyber tool.

Cyber Tools as Virtual Appliances

Some cyber tools are delivered as virtual appliances. A virtual appliance can be very favorable from a licensing perspective. Pay close attention to the virtual appliance and the related cost. For example, will the virtual appliance operate in a free hypervisor version to an enterprise hypervisor? Is all the software self-contained within the virtual appliance, requiring no additional software?

What are the software dependencies for the cyber tools? What operating system is required to run the cyber software? Does the cyber software need a database, a specific operating system, perhaps the cyber software requires an enterprise-level version of the server operating system? What are the other cyber software dependencies? What are the costs associated with all dependencies to support the cyber software? What is the reoccurring annual cost for maintenance and support of the software products?

Hardware to support existing cyber tools	Current	BAP	Savings with BAP
Cost of the server(s) operating system to support the cyber tools	$10,000	$0	$15,500
The number of servers needed to support the cyber tools	3	1	$30,000
Cost of database server to support the cyber tools	$28,000	$0.00	$28,000

Cost of other software to support the cyber tool?	$5,000	$0.00	$5,000
Cost of virtualization software to support the cyber tool	$15,000	$0.00	$15,000
Cost of high availability software to support the cyber tool or other software (database, key management)	$9,000	$0	$9,000
Cost of all cyber tools used within the environment that BAP may be able to replace, to include maintenance cost	$100,000	$0	$100,000
BAP cost is directly related to the number of controls. The price will be based on 263 controls (FISMA Moderate) and is an annual cost	$0	$78,000	$<78,000>
Maintenance cost for year 2 and year 3 (based at 15% annual cost)	$50,100	$156,000	$<106,000>
Total budget savings with BAP		$18,500	

Preparing the Environment

What preparatory software needs to be installed before the installation of the cyber software? For example, the cyber software requires a specific operating system version or a database to be installed. Make a note of the time needed for the installation as well as the skill set required. Does this expertise exist within your organization or will this be a services engagement with a third-party? Historically, installation services are a short-term engagement ranging from one week to multiple months. What is the cost to install the preparatory software so that the cyber software will run correctly?

Virtualization Software

Virtualization software may include, for example, VMWare or Microsoft. Does the cyber software tool require virtualization software? What level of virtualization software can be used? Can the cyber software run on a free version of virtualization software? What is the cost of the virtualization software?

In many environments, a virtual infrastructure may already be in place. To calculate the cost, you must understand the cost of each virtual machine. The cost of a virtual machine is typically based on the amount of "virtual RAM, virtual CPU cores and virtual disk" used to support the cyber tool. Each of the virtual machines has an associated cost.

Redundancy

Does the cyber software tool require a redundant system? What is the cost of the redundant system as well as the high availability software for the cyber software or the cyber software's dependent software?

Installation Services

How long does it take to install the cyber software? Remember that the time to install the cyber software differs from the time to configure the software. Make a note of the time required for the installation as well as the labor skill level needed. Does this labor expertise exist within your organization or will this be a service engagement with a third-party? If contracting with a third party, be aware of the length of this engagement and associated cost. Historically, installation services are a short-term engagement ranging from one week to multiple months. What is the cost to install the cyber software?

Installation Services	Current	BAP	Savings with BAP
Using an (2) internal resource, how many hours will be required for the resources to install all cyber tools? Time should include installation of hardware and software.	180	1	179 hours of labor
What is the hourly cost of the internal resource? (i.e.: $150,000/yr. is $87/hr. when considering hours and 20% burden cost)	$87.00	$87.00	
Total Cost	$13,920	$87.00	$13,833

Configuration Services

The configuration of the software is interpreted as the cyber software becoming functional within the environment. Make a note of the time required for the initial setup, as well as the skill set needed.

How much time is required for the continual optimization of the configuration? Does this expertise exist within your organization or will there be a services engagement with a third-party to complete the effort? Historically, configuration services can quickly become a staff augmentation exercise with long-term service engagements. What is the cost to configure the cyber software?

Configuration Services	Current	BAP	Savings with BAP
Using an (2) internal resource, how many hours will be required for the resources to configure all cyber tools?	320	10	310 hours of labor
What is the hourly cost of the internal resource? (i.e.: $150,000/yr. is $87/hr.	$87.00	$87.00	

when considering hours and 20% burden cost)			
Total Cost	$27,840	$870.00	$26,970

Control Development Services

What is the time required to develop your cyber standards, often referred to as cyber controls? In many organizations, the development of standards is completed by the risk management and compliance teams.

Configuration Services	Current	BAP	Savings with BAP
Using an (2) internal resource, how many hours will be required for the resources to customize the controls, group into policies, etc. (i.e. 2 controls per hour, with 263 controls we will need 131 hours. BAP automates much of the process)	262	50	81 hours of labor
What is the hourly cost of the internal resource? (i.e.: $150,000/yr. is $87/hr. when considering hours and 20% burden cost)	$116.00	$116.00	
Total Cost	$30,392	$5,800	$24,592

The development of your cyber standards *does not include the implementation of the cyber standards*, only the development of the standards into policy. For some environments, this may include a fresh start to develop the cyber standards whereas others may be modifying existing cyber standards. The development of your cyber standards will include the adjustment of the implementation language. The development of your cyber standards should reveal the utilization of your existing cyber software. In most cases, if you are utilizing cyber software that does not support your cyber standards, careful consideration as to the value of this cyber software should be evaluated.

Risk Management and SOC

Risk management of the cyberinfrastructure often includes a security operation center (SOC). Is your security operation center managed internally or are you leveraging a contracted service? If your security operation center is managed internally, you need to calculate the cost for the security operation center space, power, hardware, software, and staff. If your security operation center is a contracted service, you need to include the cost of that service as well.

Risk Management (Cyber Operations, SOC)	Current	BAP	Savings with BAP
Using internal SOC resources, how many resources are used in SOC operations?	20	12	Re-allocate 8 of 20 SOC staff
What is the hourly cost of the internal resource? (i.e.: $150,000/yr. is $87/hr. when considering hours and 20% burden cost)	$102.00	$102.00	
What is the one-time standup cost for power, hardware, software and space to support the SOC?	$20,000	$10.000	$10,000
Total labor cost to support the SOC	$4,204,400	$2,416,381.15	$1,788,018.85

Cyber Health of your Controls?

Is your security operation center providing you with the cyber health of your controls or are they remediating and preventing known threat without correlation to the health of the security standards implemented? Most security operation centers use technology to discover and deter known threat to the environment, assessment of risk priority and remediation. What is the cost for your security operations? For some situations, this may be the calculation of the help desk staff member or a fractional cost of an individual performing multiple tasks.

Remediation

As a threat occurs, the SOC analysts investigate the event to remediate as soon as possible. The investigation includes understanding the threat.

Remediation of the event

Remediation is the ability to resolve the event. Seek automation to track events, based on actual events in the environment. Time and cost savings are recognized with the automation and management of the events.

Risk Management (Cyber Operations, SOC)	Current	BAP	Savings with BAP
How many security threats are received per day?	7		BAP provides an AI to ascertain security threat
What is the average time, in minutes to investigate the threat?	90	60	30 minutes saved per threat

What is the average time, in minutes to prepare the remediation paperwork?	30	15	15 minutes saved per threat
What is the hourly cost of the internal resource? (i.e.: $150,000/yr. is $87/hr. when considering hours and 20% burden cost)	$116	$116	
Number of hours per month (based on 30 days per month) to resolve and document threat	420	262.5	157.5
Monthly cost to investigate and complete the remediation tasks and paperwork (based on a 30 day month of 210 threats per month)	$48,720	$30,450	$18,270

Appendix A: Firewall Breach

The firewall breach has a ripple effect on multiple components within the system, as well as controls you selected for Cyber. Each control within Cyber has a different risk score based on weights and priorities, calculations that exceed the functionality of SIEM and Log Aggregation. Cyber Accountability is the complete view of the system (hardware, software in your environment) that includes understanding all the risks, cumulatively for all impacted components.

BAP uniquely analyzes the impact to all the controls in the policy to provide an accurate representation of the health of your Cyber controls and policies. **BAP** provides Accountable Security. Please contact info@bapsolution.com for more information.

Appendix A provides potential controls that may be impacted by the firewall breach. The list is dependent upon your environment.

Access Control, Controls

The following represent the access control, controls that may be impacted by the breach. All of which impact the environment at different levels.

Control	Security Objective	Potential impact to the environment
AC-2 (6)	Account management-dynamic privilege management	Modification of the account privilege management will have a cascade impact on all systems
AC-2 (7)	Account management-rule-based schemes	Modification of the account privilege management will have a cascade impact on all systems
AC-3	Access enforcement	Modification of the account privilege management will have a cascade impact on all systems
AC-3 (3)	Access enforcement-mandatory access control	Modification of the account privilege management will have a cascade impact on all systems
AC-3 (4)	Access enforcement-discretionary access control	Modification of the account privilege management will have a cascade impact on all systems
AC-3 (5)	Access enforcement-security relevant information	The access control system risk or increases because of the firewall penetration. Modification to the rules established may play sensitive, relevant security information at risk

AC-3 (7)	Access enforcement-role-based access control	Modification of the account privilege management will have a cascade impact on all systems
AC-3 (8)	Access enforcement-revocation of access authorizations	Unauthorized access to the revocation/authorization objectives for the organization can create unwanted and unknown access to sensitive information
AC-3 (10)	access enforcement-audited override of access control mechanisms	change to the audit logging and the environment will be difficult to know who is doing what on the system
AC-4 (15)	information flow enforcement-detection of unsanctioned information	altering the parameters because of unauthorized access will disable desired information flow enforcement
AC-17	remote access	unauthorized users may be granted remote access to the system
AC-18	wireless access	modification to the wireless security can find rogue devices within the system
AC-19	access control for mobile devices	with the growing amount of data on mobile devices unauthorized access may create a substantial impact
AC-20	use of external information systems	modifications to controls for rent external information systems may lead to loss of sensitive data

Audit, Configuration, Identity and Maintenance Controls

The following represent the controls from audit, configuration, identity and maintenance control families that may be impacted by the breach. All of which impact the environment at different levels.

Control	Security Objective	Potential impact to the environment
AU-9 (4)	Protection of audit information-access by subset of privileged users	Change the audit logging in the environment will be difficult to know who is doing what on the system
AU-13	Monitoring for information disclosure	Monitoring can be disabled when a threat is present
CM-6 (2)	Configuration settings-respond to unauthorized changes	Safeguards can be modified by unauthorized users because of the security breach
CM-7 (4)	Least functionality-unauthorized software and blacklisting	Unauthorized software application list is modified to allow harmful applications in the environment
CM-8 (3)	Information system component inventory-automated unauthorized component detection	Component inventory can be modified to include harmful components to the environment
IA-2 (12)	Identification and authentication (organizational users)-acceptance of PIV credentials	PIV credentials can be modified by unauthorized individual
IA-12	Identity proofing	User identity information can be falsely modified
IR-4	Incident handling	Harmful incidents can be silenced and ignored

		creating risk to the environment
MA-5 (1)	Maintenance personnel-individuals without appropriate access	Personnel security clearances can be modified by unauthorized access
MA-5 (2)	Maintenance personnel-security clearances for classified systems	Access to classified systems can be granted to unauthorized individuals
MP-2	Media access	Rogue media restrictions and safeguards can be disabled
MP-4 (2)	Media storage-automated restricted access	Access to media storage areas can be granted by unauthorized individuals

Physical Access, Program Management, Risk Assessment, System and Communication Protection Controls

The following represent the controls from Physical Access, Program Management, Risk Assessment, System and Communication Protection control families that may be impacted by the breach. All of which impact the environment at different levels.

Control	Security Objective	Potential impact to the environment
PE-2	Physical access authorizations	Contractors and employees can be given physical access without proper authorization
PE-2 (1)	Physical access authorizations-access by position and role	Positions and rolls can be modified to allow for unauthorized access
PE-3	Physical access control	Physical access authentication, verification

		audit logs can be modified without proper authority
PE-3 (1)	Physical access control-information system access	Physical access authorization to facility and systems can be modified by unauthorized individual
PE-5	Access control for output devices	Unauthorized individuals can be given access to obtain sensitive information output
PE-8	Visitor access records	Visitor record logs can be changed by unauthorized individual
PM-27	Individual access control	Privacy act system of records checkpoints can be altered by unauthorized individuals
PS-6 (2)	Access agreements-classified information requiring special protection	Access to classified information can be modified by unauthorized individual
RA-5 (5)	Vulnerability scanning-privileged access	Vulnerability scanning result can be modified and present risk
SC-4	Information in shared resource	Information sharing access can be modified by unauthorized individual
SC-5 (1)	Denial of service protection-restricted internal users	Provide the ability for individuals to launch denial of service attacks against other systems

Document ideas about your Strategy

www.ingramcontent.com/pod-product-compliance
Lightning Source LLC
Chambersburg PA
CBHW051215050326
40689CB00008B/1314